NOISY
BOOKS

For John Joe and Sam – PH

First published 2007
Evans Brothers Limited
2A Portman Mansions
Chiltern Street
London W1U 6NR

British Library Cataloguing in Publication Data

Harrison, Paul, 1969-
    Noisy books. - (Twisters)
    1. Children's stories
    I. Title
    823.9'2[J]

ISBN: 978 0237 53468 4 (hb)
ISBN: 978 0237 53467 7 (pb)

Printed in China

Series Editor: Nick Turpin
Design: Robert Walster
Production: Jenny Mulvanny

NOISY BOOKS

Paul Harrison
and Fabiano Fiorin

Evans

I love the
quiet library.

And all its noisy books.

7

"ROAR!" goes the dinosaur.

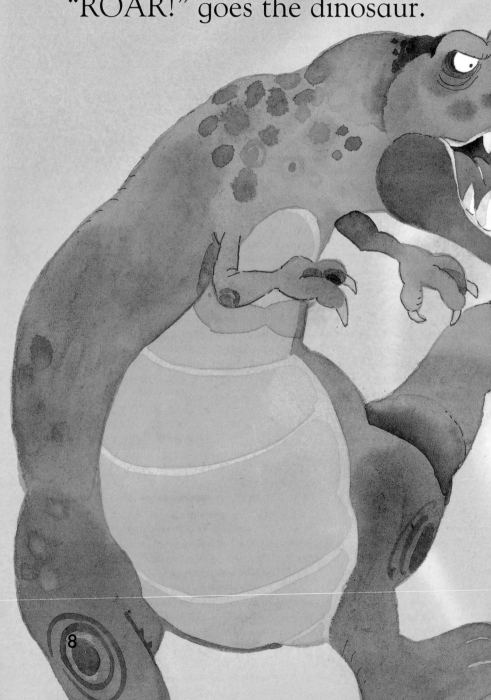

8

"Shh!" says Mum.

"BOOM!" goes the cannon.

"Shh!" says Mum.

"WHOO!" goes the ghost.

17

"Shh!" says Mum.

"ZAP!" goes the alien.

"Shh!" says Mum.

Home time.

"WHOOPS!" goes Mum.

"THUD" go the books.

"Shh!" I say.

Why not try reading another Twisters book?